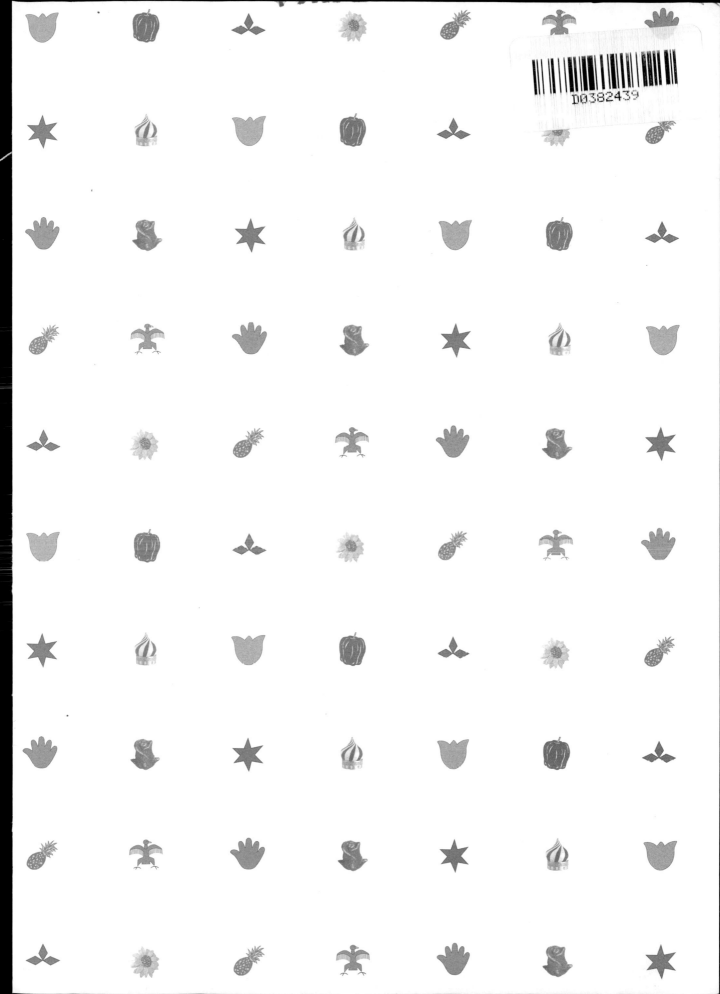

Papier Mâché
made easy

Papier Mâché

made easy

Series Editors: Susan & Martin Penny

David & Charles

A DAVID & CHARLES BOOK

First published in the UK in 1999

A catalogue record for this book is available from the British Library.

ISBN 0 7153 0932 3

Series Editors: Susan & Martin Penny
Designed and produced by Penny & Penny
Illustrations: Fred Fieber at Red Crayola
Photography: Jon Stone

Printed in Italy by L.E.G.O. S.p.A.
for David & Charles
Brunel House Newton Abbot Devon

Contents

Introduction to Papier Mâché

Papier Mâché Made Easy is a complete guide to the craft of papier mâché; no expensive equipment is needed to get started, just a supply of recycled newspaper and PVA glue. Begin with a simple project like the gift bowls on page 50, where you will soon learn the basic techniques needed to produce beautifully moulded paper pieces

Essential equipment

Below is a list of equipment needed when working with papier mâché:

- **Mixing bowl** – used for mixing paper pulp.
- **Strainer or sieve** – used to strain excess water from paper pulp.
- **Liquidizer or blender** – used for breaking paper down into pulp.
- **Strong plastic bag** – used for mixing ready-mixed paper pulp.
- **Clingfilm** – used for wrapping around a mould before adding the pulp.
- **Paper** – use copier paper to make a tracing of the design.
- **Decorator's paintbrush** – used for applying varnish.
- **Paintbrush** – used for applying PVA to newspaper pieces.
- **Newspaper** – used for covering your work surface.
- **Kitchen paper** – for cleaning equipment.
- **Rubber gloves** – to protect your hands when colouring paper pulp with dye.
- **Soft cloth and spoon** – for pressing paper pulp into a mould.
- **Cutting knife** – used for cutting a cardboard framework for making trays and boxes.
- **Masking tape** – used for joining cardboard.
- **Sandpaper** – used for rubbing down the surface of papier mâché.
- **Jam jar** – used for storing dilute PVA

Making paper pulp

Below is a list of consumables that you will need when making pulp:

- **Cartridge paper** – white or coloured can be used to make paper pulp.
- **Brown paper, sugar paper, handmade paper and newspaper** – any decorative or coloured paper that will break down when soaked overnight in water can also be used.

- **Ready-mixed paper pulp** – white or off white substance that is mixed with water to make pulp. Bought from craft shops, as a fine powder or a more fibrous mix; blend with water and a little washing-up liquid for a user-friendly pulp.
- **PVA glue** – mix with the sieved pulp in the proportions of approximately 15g (¹/₂oz) glue to 250g (¹/₂lb) pulp.
- **Washing-up liquid** – blend with pulp for a more malleable mix.
- **Water** – soak the paper overnight in water, then add more water to the mix before blending into a pulp.
- **Cold water fabric dye** – used to colour pulp.

Layered papier mâché

Below is a list of consumables that you will need for applying paper strips:

● **Newspaper** – although other fine paper can be used, newspaper makes the best layered papier mâché.

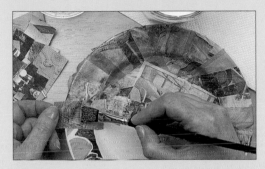

● **PVA glue** – paste the strips of newspaper using a mix of 3 parts PVA to 1 part water.
● **Petroleum jelly** – rub over the mould to stop the paper layers sticking to it.

Useful hints and tips

✔ Add plenty of water when blending pulp
✔ It is easier to make small quantities of pulp
✔ Remove excess water from the prepared pulp
✔ Use your hands to mix PVA into the pulp
✔ Adding washing-up liquid to ready-mixed pulp will make it more malleable
✔ Mixed paper pulp can be kept in the refrigerator if sealed in a plastic bag
✔ Use plenty of PVA when pasting paper layers
✔ Brush out air bubbles under the paper layers

Painting papier mâché

✔ Prime papier mâché with white emulsion or acrylic gesso before painting
✔ Use emulsion, acrylic, gouache, powder or metallic paint
✔ Seal with matt or gloss acrylic varnish

Which mould?

Almost anything can be used as a mould when making papier mâché, as long as you remember to use a barrier to stop the paper sticking to the mould. Below are some of the points to consider when choosing the right mould to work with.

● **China or plastic bowls and platters**
　Used for making bowl shapes and plates
　Almost anything can be used as a mould
　Use with pulp or paper strips
　Cover with petroleum jelly and clingfilm before applying the pulp
　Spread with petroleum jelly if using paper strips
　Build up at least 15 layers of paper strips
● **Card, mounting board and corrugated**
　Used for constructing boxes and trays
　Use masking tape to reinforce the joins and for piecing the cardboard together
　Cover with pasted paper, building up the layers over the cardboard
● **Aluminium foil**
　Scrunch up to make a core for a ball or cone shape
　Cover with PVA before adding pulp or paper layers
　Can be sanded for a smooth finish
● **Fruit and vegetables**
　Use real fruit and vegetables as a mould to make fake fruit shapes and caskets
　Cover with petroleum jelly before adding at least 10 layers of paper
　The paper fruit has to be cut in half to remove the real fruit
　Can be sanded until smooth
● **Lampshade**
　Use as a mould when making a conical shaped vase
　The metal frame needs to be removed
　The lampshade will form part of the finished structure
　Apply at least 10 layers of paper
● **Balloon**
　Makes very good bowl shape
　Build up at least 15 layers of paper

Making Paper Pulp

Paper is the essential ingredient for papier mâché; you can make it from plain white cartridge paper, or you can use newspaper, brown paper, sugar paper or handmade textured paper for interesting effects. If you would rather not make your own pulp, ready-mixed dry paper pulp is easy to use and available at most good craft shops

Handmade pulp

1 Tear paper into narrow strips and then into pieces of about 2.5cm (1in) square, then leave to soak overnight in a bowl of water. Cartridge paper makes good pulp, but any paper that will break down when left to soak overnight in water can be used.

2 Add plenty of water to the mix, then use a hand blender or liquidizer to break down the paper into pulp. It will make it easier if you work with small quantities of pulp.

3 Strain the prepared pulp over a bowl to remove the excess water, then press the water from the pulp using a spoon; or use your hand to squeeze out the remaining water. The pulp should resemble a damp spongy mass when ready.

4 Mix PVA glue with the sieved pulp using your hands, in the proportions of approximately 15g (½oz) glue to 250g (½lb) pulp. The mixture is now ready to use.

Ready-mixed pulp

1 Paper pulp can be bought from most craft shops, as a fine powder or as a more fibrous mix, ready to be mixed with water. Read the instructions on the pack for the correct quantities of pulp to water; glue should not be added unless stated on the packet. Place the pulp in a strong plastic bag, then add the water: warm water will help to speed up the mixing process.

2 Add a small amount of washing-up liquid to the pulp/water mix. This will make the pulp more malleable and easier to use. Tie a knot in the bag, then knead thoroughly, until all the powder has disappeared and the pulp is smooth in consistency.

Dyed paper pulp

To colour prepared pulp make up cold water fabric dye, following the manufacturers' instructions. Add a few drops of dye to the pulp then leave for several hours before squeezing out the excess. Water-soluble paint can also be used to dye the pulp, but the colours will be less intense.

Coloured paper pulp

Coloured cartridge paper, sugar paper, brown paper and newsprint can also be used to make paper pulp. It should be treated in the same way as white paper: tearing, then soaking in water, before straining, blending and mixing with PVA glue. When dry it will not be as strong in colour as dyed pulp.

Using Paper Pulp

Moulded pulp gives a very different texture to laid paper strips: it is rough in appearance but has a naive charm that is very difficult to achieve in any other medium. Once the coloured or white paper has been made into pulp it can be moulded over or in almost any container, from a serving bowl to a sweet mould.

Moulding over a container

1 Almost any container can be used as a mould for paper pulp. Grease the mould with petroleum jelly, then wrap in clingfilm. Place lumps of prepared white or coloured papier mâché pulp firmly on to the mould, making a thin even layer.

3 Before painting, a white paper bowl should be primed with two coats of white emulsion or acrylic gesso: this will give a good basecoat for the paint. Decorate the bowl with acrylic paint then finish with two coats of gloss or matt acrylic varnish.

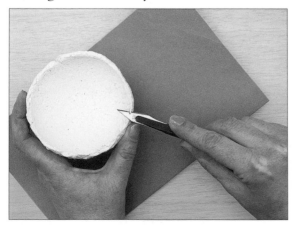

2 When the pulp is dry ease the paper bowl from the mould, and peel off the clingfilm. Use a sharp knife to tidy the top of the bowl, then finish with sandpaper.

4 Paper pulp can also be moulded inside a bowl. Grease with petroleum jelly then wrap in clingfilm before pressing the pulp well down into the bowl with a spoon.

Using plastic sweet moulds

1 Brush neat washing-up liquid over the inside of each mould, getting it well down into the corners. Press a small amount of prepared paper pulp into the mould; turn the mould over and check there are no air bubbles in the pulp, then fill level with the top. When dry the paper shapes will shrink away from the sides of the mould and can be tipped out.

2 Using sharp scissors cut away any excess paper that surrounds the paper shapes, then finish the edges with fine sandpaper. Prime the shapes with white emulsion or gesso before decorating with acrylic paint. Seal the surface with a coat of gloss or matt acrylic varnish.

Using aluminium foil

Aluminium foil can be used to make shapes, like balls and cones, because of the lightness of the material. A coat of dilute PVA glue on the foil will help the papier mâché pulp to stick; press the pulp on to the wet glue, moulding it well in place. When the pulp is dry it can be sanded, and painted.

Using a template

A template can be placed under clingfilm as a guide for moulding coloured paper pulp on to a bowl. Attach the templates with double sided tape, then rub the bowl with petroleum jelly before wrapping in clingfilm. Work the patterned areas first, then fill in the background, moulding the colours together.

Using Paper Strips

Almost anything can be used as a mould for newspaper strips as long as it is covered with clingfilm and/or petroleum jelly to stop the paper sticking to it. Use dilute PVA glue to apply the newspaper; the smaller the strips, and the more layers you apply, the better the finished effect will be

Pasting over a dish

Rub petroleum jelly over the surface of a plate. Paste on strips of newspaper using a mix of 3 parts PVA to 1 part water; apply 15 layers. Leave to dry then ease from the plate.

Pasting over fruit

Rub petroleum jelly over the surface of a fruit or vegetable, then paste layers of newspaper over the surface. When dry, cut in half and remove the fruit or vegetable in one piece.

Pasting over a lampshade

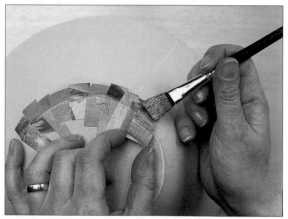

To make a conical shaped bowl: remove the fittings from inside a lampshade, then stick a card circle over one end. Paste newspaper strips over the surface, building up the layers.

Using coloured paper

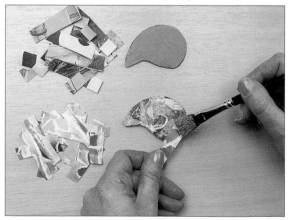

Coloured paper can be used instead of paint to decorate papier mâché. When the newspaper is dry, apply a final layer of giftwrap or tissue paper strips using diluted PVA glue.

Pasting over a balloon

1 A quick and easy way to make a footed bowl is to use a balloon as a mould. To make the bowl base, tape a strip of cardboard into a ring, then cover the bottom with a card circle. Paste strips of newspaper overlapping the join between the ring and the base circle, using diluted PVA glue; leave to dry. Blow up a balloon and sit it smaller end down into a flower pot.

2 Place the base on top of the balloon. Apply five layers of newspaper strips to the base and lower third of the balloon; leave to dry. Pop the balloon and remove it from the paper bowl. Using sharp scissors cut the upper edge of the bowl level. Prime with white emulsion or gesso then decorate.

Pasting over cardboard

1 Build your tray or box shape from corrugated cardboard, held together with pieces of masking tape. Use a cutting board and sharp knife to cut the card, making sure the pieces are exactly the right size or they will not fit perfectly together. Fit the shorter sides, then the longer, overlapping the base and shorter sides. Use masking tape on the edges to keep the sides square.

2 Paste small strips of newspaper over the joins and the corners of the cardboard using dilute PVA glue. Smooth the pieces down, removing all air bubbles. Build up the layers over the cardboard, overlapping the edges of the paper: each layer should be laid in a different direction for strength.

Sunflowers and Vase

This stylish vase and bright sunflowers are simply made from cardboard, which is then covered with layers of papier mâché made from newspaper and toilet tissue. If you would like to make other flowers like daisies or gerberas, cut the petal template slightly smaller and then paint the finished petals white, orange or bright pink

You will need

- Stiff mounting board – 30x40cm (12x16in)
- White paper, white card, crêpe paper
- Newspapers, toilet tissue
- Acrylic paint – bright yellow, green
- Acrylic lustre paint – turquoise, deep blue, petrol blue, gold
- Emulsion paint – white
- PVA glue, water
- Peppercorns
- Thin florist's wire, thick covered wire
- Florist's tape – green
- Scissors, pencil
- Masking tape, blunt knife
- Glue brush, paintbrush
- Container for mixing glue

Making the templates

1 Trace the sunflower petal on page 19 on to white paper using a pencil. Cut out the template and draw around the shape on to white card; cut out the petal. Using this petal cut 24 petals for each flower head from the white card.

2 Make a card template of the calyx and cut the shape twice from green crêpe paper for each flower.

3 For the flower centres, cut two 5cm (2in) circles, one from white card and one from mounting board.

Forming the petals

1 To make a petal, cut a 12cm (5in) length of fine florist's wire for each petal. Fold in half and attach to one side of a petal shape, protruding from the blunt end.

2 Tear the toilet tissue into sections: one section will be sufficient to cover a petal. Dip the toilet tissue into water; lightly squeeze to remove excess water, then wrap the tissue around the card petal covering the wire and the card. Fold in any tissue that is beyond the card shape. The paper will bond to itself when dry, as long as you squeeze it firmly together when wet. Slightly curl the petal: the wire will hold the petal in shape. Leave to dry for several days.

3 Wrap moist toilet tissue around the 5cm (2in) card circle. This will form the centre front of the sunflower. Build up the layers until it is 5mm (¼in) thick. Squeeze out the excess water, then allow to dry.

4 Paint 20 petals with bright yellow acrylic paint and four with green. For the orange tipped sunflower, paint the petals yellow, then brush orange paint on to the tips, blending it towards the base. Paint both sides of the flower centre using gold lustre paint.

Assembling the sunflower

1 Take the 5cm (2in) circle cut from mounting board. To make the sunflower stem: fold the end of a 30cm (12in) length of thick covered wire into a 2cm (1in) loop. Attach the wire loop to the back of the mounting board circle using PVA glue. Paste several layers of toilet tissue over the wire loop to hold it in place. Leave to dry.

2 Each sunflower should have approximately 20 petals and four leaves, which are secured to the front of the mounting board circle, working in layers, from the back to the front, with each petal curling downwards.

3 For the back petal layer, place two yellow and one green petal on the mounting board circle, with the wire ends facing inwards, and the petals overlapping the circle by 5mm (¼in). Place a small piece of toilet tissue over the wire ends, then brush the tissue with PVA glue. Repeat this process until you have a circle of eight yellow and four green evenly spaced petals; allow to dry.

4 Add the next layer of seven yellow petals in the same way as the first, positioning them slightly further in towards the centre of the flower. Try to arrange the petals so that they overlap the petals on the first layer, securing them as before with glued toilet tissue.

5 Glue a final layer of five petals evenly spaced around the flowerhead. Place a piece of dry toilet tissue over the wires in the centre of the sunflower and apply a coat of PVA glue. Add several more layers of tissue, then allow to dry.

6 Make a hole in the centre of each calyx-shaped crêpe paper piece. Spread glue over the back of the sunflower centre, then thread the crêpe paper on to the stem, positioning it on to the glue; attach the second calyx in the same way.

7 Wrap a length of green florist's tape down the length of the wire stem.

8 Turn the sunflower over and glue the gold painted circle over the centre of the sunflower, covering the wired petal ends. Glue peppercorns to the centre of the sunflower for decoration. Bend the sunflower heads slightly forward.

Building the vase

1 Trace over the templates for the vase on page 19 using white paper.

2 Cut out the templates, then lay the vase side template on to stiff mounting board and draw around the shape. Lift off the template and reposition next to the already drawn shape, with long sides touching. Draw around and repeat once more: you will have three shapes drawn directly next to each other.

3 Following the trace on page 19, draw in the dividing lines to make a six segmented vase shape. Cut out the vase shape, then using a blunt knife, score down the five internal lines. Fold the vase on the scored lines until the edges butt together: try to get a close fit but any small imperfections will be concealed when the papier mâché is applied.

4 Lay the hexagon-shaped base template on to the mounting board; draw around the shape and cut out. Fix the base to the bottom of the vase using masking tape.

Applying the papier mâché

1 Tear strips of newspaper into pieces approximately 3x4cm (1½x2in).

2 Mix equal quantities of PVA glue and water in a container, then paint a coat of the PVA glue mix on to the inside and outside of the vase; leave to dry.

3 Brush a small area on the outside of the vase with glue and lay a newspaper piece on top. Brush with more glue and place another strip slightly overlapping the first. Continue adding paper pieces until the outer surface is completely covered. Make sure that the edges of the newspaper pieces are not directly on the folds of the vase. Allow to dry for several hours.

4 Add another layer of newspaper pieces; leave to dry. Continue adding layers until the joins and the surface of the vase are neat and well covered.

Painting the vase

1 When the papier mâché is completely dry, paint the inside and outside of the vase with a coat of white emulsion: this will give a good base coat for the paint.

2 When the emulsion is dry, apply a coat of acrylic turquoise lustre paint to the inside of the vase. Leave to dry and then paint the outside of the vase with the same colour.

3 When the paint is dry, brush petrol blue paint two thirds of the way up the outside of the vase: let the brush strokes feather out over the turquoise paint.

4 Turn the vase upside down and paint the vase bottom using deep blue; continue the paint up the sides of the vase covering the bottom third. Feather the edges of the paint as before, this will give you three graduated layers of colour: deep blue at the bottom, petrol blue in the middle and turquoise at the top.

5 When the paint is dry, add flecks of gold acrylic paint randomly over the outside surface of the vase; leave to dry.

6 Arrange your sunflowers in the vase. For extra stability pack glass marbles or pebbles around the flower stems.

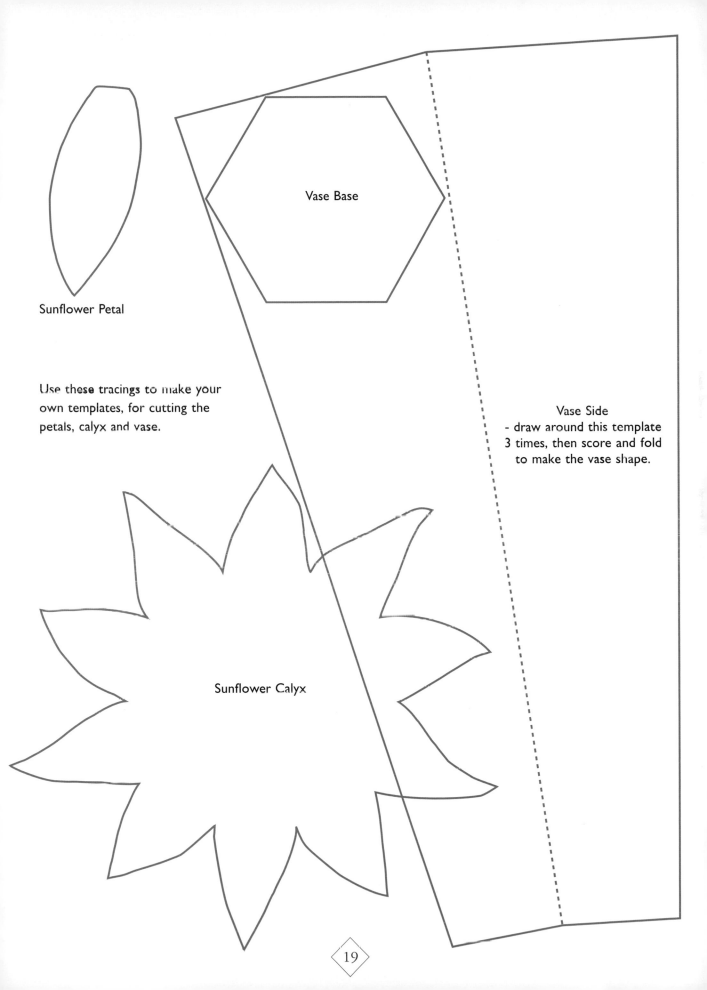

Sunflower Petal

Vase Base

Use these tracings to make your own templates, for cutting the petals, calyx and vase.

Vase Side
- draw around this template 3 times, then score and fold to make the vase shape.

Sunflower Calyx

Caribbean Platter and Bowl

Bright colours and simple lines have been used to create a platter and bowl with a truly tropical feel. The classic shapes are easy to achieve, as the papier mâché has been moulded over a china plate and bowl, using many layers of newspaper. Once dry the paper platter can be removed and painted

Although almost any paper can be used to create papier mâché layers, newspaper is the easiest to use and will give the best finish.

You will need
- Newspapers
- PVA glue, water
- China bowl
- China serving platter
- Emulsion paint – white
- Acrylic paint – light green, bright blue, dark green, gold
- Scissors, pencil
- Washing-up liquid, soft cloth
- Petroleum jelly, jam jar
- Glue brush, paintbrush
- Acrylic varnish – clear gloss

Preparing the platter

1 Rub a generous layer of petroleum jelly over the top surface of the china platter. Smooth it with your finger to ensure total coverage. This will allow the paper platter to be easily removed when it is dry.

Making the platter

1 In a jam jar dilute three parts PVA glue in one part of water to make the paste.

2 Tear the newspaper into strips about 10cm (4in) long and 2.5cm (1in) wide. Brush paste on to both sides of the newspaper strips then place them on the platter, overlapping as you go, until the platter is covered (see Using Paper Strips, page 12). Repeat the process, applying about 15 layers. Make sure that you apply even layers across the whole of the platter, or it may become weak and distorted in parts when dry. Leave the papier mâché platter for 48 hours or until completely dry.

Attaching the palm leaves

1 For each leaf on the platter you will need to cut ten identical leaf shapes from newspaper. Use the large template on page 23 just as a guide, varying the shape and size of the leaves across the platter.

2 Paste a leaf shape on to the platter using the PVA solution, then paste the other nine

layers on top. Repeat for the other leaves. Leave for 48 hours or until dry.

Removing the paper platter

1 When dry carefully ease the rim of the paper platter from the china mould, then peel it away.

2 Clean the underside of the paper platter with a damp cloth and washing-up liquid to remove any traces of petroleum jelly. Trim the edge with scissors, following the line of the rim on the underside.

Decorating the platter

1 Apply a coat of white emulsion paint over the entire paper platter and leave to dry. If the coverage is not good, apply another coat: this will provide a smooth surface for painting.

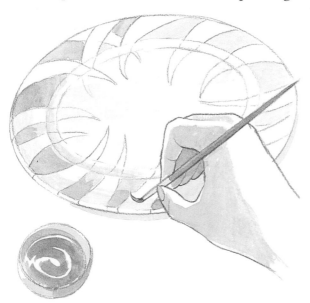

2 Paint bright blue around the outer edge of the platter, blending it on to the white central area, but avoiding the leaf shapes. Leave to dry.

3 Finally paint the leaves with the dark and light green using the photograph on

page 21 as a guide. Apply the light green first over the whole of the leaf, then use the dark green paint along the lower edges, to give the leaves a three-dimensional look.

4 Allow the paint to dry for several days then apply two thin coats of acrylic varnish over the whole platter. Allow the varnish to dry between layers. This will give the platter a tough shiny surface.

Preparing the bowl

1 Rub a generous layer of petroleum jelly inside the bowl. Smooth it with your finger to ensure total coverage.

2 Tear up the newspaper into strips as before. You should have enough strips to complete at least 15 layers.

Making the bowl

1 Begin pasting the newspaper strips into the bowl, using the PVA glue and water mix. Paste them vertically around the bowl, making sure that each strip overlaps and they are applied evenly over the surface in the same way as the platter on page 20. Build up about 15 layers.

2 Leave the bowl for 48 hours or until dry, then carefully remove from the china bowl.

Clean away the petroleum jelly with a damp cloth and some washing-up liquid. If you do not remove all the petroleum jelly the paint will not adhere to the surface.

Creating the decoration

1 Using the template as a guide, cut leaf shapes from newspaper. For each leaf you will need to cut ten identical leaf shapes. Paste the leaves evenly in the criss-cross pattern, around the bowl. Build up the layers for the lower leaf of each pair first, then apply the top leaf in the same way. Leave for 48 hours or until dry.

2 Paint the bowl with a base coat of white emulsion paint. When dry, paint inside the bowl with gold acrylic paint; leave to dry. Paint bright blue on the base and partially up the sides of the bowl, fading it into the white.

3 Paint the leaves two-tone green, with the darkest areas on the lower side of each leaf.

4 Allow the paint to dry for several days then apply two thin coats of acrylic varnish over the bowl. Allow the varnish to dry between layers. This will seal the bowl and give it a shiny finish.

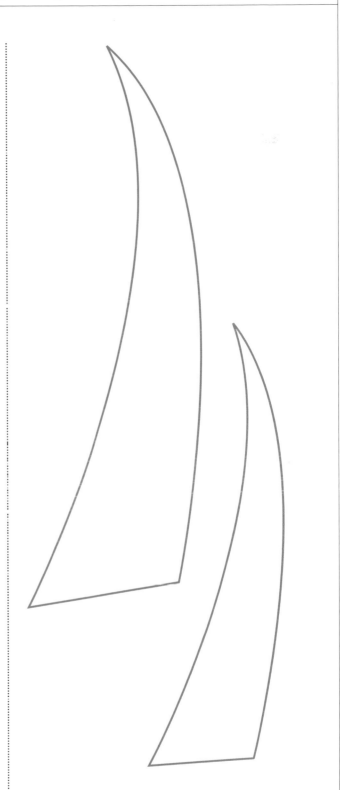

Use these shapes as guides to cut leaves from newspaper. Vary the shape and size of the leaves to suit the style of platter and bowl you are using.

Native American Trays

Geometric shapes, arrows, a bird and feathers in the style of painting found on Indian artefacts give these rectangular trays a Native American feel. The layers of newspaper and brown paper have been painted, then laced with leather thonging and beads for a truly authentic look

You will need

- Corrugated card
- Newspaper
- Acrylic paint – cream, dark red, black and turquoise
- Masking tape
- Brown parcel paper, white paper, ballpoint pen, typewriter carbon paper
- PVA glue, water, container for mixing glue
- Bradawl, glue brush, paintbrush
- Water-based matt varnish
- Turquoise leather thonging
- Beads

Making the large tray

1 For the large tray, cut a rectangle of corrugated card 35.5x25cm (14x10in) and four strips of corrugated card 35.5x4.5cm (14x1¾in).

2 Using masking tape, attach the longer two strips upright against the long sides of the large rectangle. Tape the remaining two strips against the other edges of the cardboard, cutting the ends level with the ends of the first strips to form the sides of the tray. Tape the corners together using masking tape.

Applying the papier mâché

1 Tear the newspaper into 5cm (2in) wide strips. Mix the PVA glue in a container with a little water until it is the consistency of single cream.

2 Brush the PVA solution on to a newspaper strip and smooth it over the tray. Continue adding strips, overlapping the edges of the paper, and building up 10 layers: each layer should be laid in a different direction. To strengthen the corners, tear the newspaper into smaller strips and paste them smoothly around the corners.

3 Apply a final layer of brown parcel paper strips over the entire surface of the tray, then leave to dry: this may take several days.

4 Use a bradawl to make a row of holes on the sides of the tray, equidistant apart and 1cm (³⁄₈in) below the upper edge - approximately four holes on the short sides and seven holes on the long sides.

Painting the large tray

1 Thin the cream paint with a little water, then paint the base and underside of the tray, giving it a streaky finish. Thin the dark red paint in the same way, then paint the sides of the tray, inside and out.

2 Make a tracing of the large geometric design opposite on to white paper. Lay the typewriter carbon paper on the tray, shiny side down. Lay the tracing on top, then carefully draw over the design lines, transferring them to the tray. Turn the tracing around and repeat for the other half, making sure the two halves are matched up.

3 Paint the design in black, cream, dark red and turquoise following the photograph on page 25 for position. Leave to dry.

4 Paint the tray with three coats of acrylic matt varnish for protection.

5 When dry, lace the thonging through the holes, adding beads randomly. Knot the

thong ends together, thread a bead on each end and then knot together.

Making the small tray

1 For the small tray, cut a 10cm (4in) square of corrugated card, two strips 10x3cm (4x1¹⁄₄in) and two 12x3cm (5x1¹⁄₄in).

2 Tape the four strips on to the sides of the cardboard square, cutting the ends level at the corners to form the sides of the tray. Tape the corners together using masking tape.

3 Apply layers of newspaper and brown paper in the same way as for the large tray.

4 Thin the cream paint with water, then paint the base and underside of the tray, giving it a streaky finish. Paint the sides with thinned dark red paint, allow to dry.

5 Make a tracing of the bird motif below and the feather motif opposite. Use carbon paper to transfer the design lines to the tray as for the large tray: the bird on the base and a feather motif on the outside of each side. Paint the bird and feather motifs in turquoise, black, cream and dark red, following the photograph on page 25 for position. Allow to dry, then apply three coats of matt acrylic varnish to the tray for protection.

Bird Motif

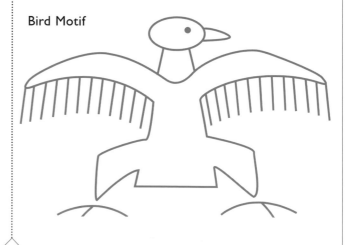

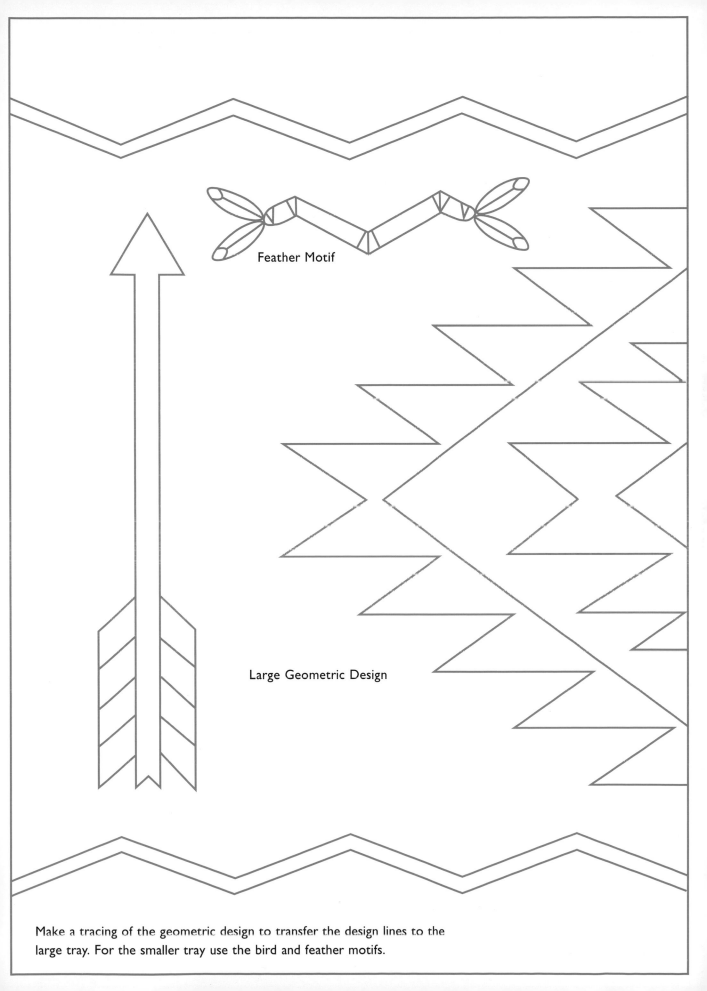

Feather Motif

Large Geometric Design

Make a tracing of the geometric design to transfer the design lines to the
large tray. For the smaller tray use the bird and feather motifs.

Rose Casket and Card

This casket would make a wonderful Valentine or anniversary gift, or you may prefer to make just the papier mâché roses and use them to create a special card or gift tag. To give the casket an extra special finish, add gold braid, beads and small brass charms

You will need

- Stiff mounting board – 30x55cm (12x22in)
- Ready-mixed papier mâché pulp
- Giftwrap tissue paper – purple, blue, pink, red, gold
- Newspaper, aluminium baking foil
- Stiff card – gold
- Emulsion paint – white
- Acrylic paint – gold, burgundy, deep red, green
- Plastic sweet moulds – hearts, roses
- Greeting card, parcel label
- Narrow braid – gold
- Small gold charms, gold thread, beads, needle
- PVA glue, water, washing-up liquid
- Scissors, pencil, white paper
- Masking tape, blunt knife, sandpaper
- Glue brush, paintbrushes
- Container for mixing glue
- Water-based matt acrylic varnish

Making the hearts and roses

1 Make a quantity of papier mâché using ready-mixed paper pulp or make your own paper pulp (see Making Paper Pulp, page 8).

2 Rub the inside of the heart and rose sweet moulds with neat washing-up liquid to prevent the papier mâché sticking to the plastic.

3 Press a small quantity of pulp into the mould. Turn the mould over to check that the shape is filled with pulp and there are no air bubbles. Keep adding lumps of pulp until the mould is filled; smooth the surface, then leave to dry for several days.

4 When the papier mâché shapes are completely dry they will shrink away from

the edges of the mould, and can be tipped out. Neaten the edges of each shape with scissors or a knife, then rub the back on sandpaper to make a flat surface for attaching to the casket.

Painting the hearts and roses

1 Apply two coats of red paint to the hearts and roses. Paint the leaves on the roses green and then add detail to the rose petals using burgundy paint. Allow to dry then highlight some areas with gold paint to emphasise the shape.

Making the casket

1 Trace over the templates for the casket on pages 32-35 on to white paper.

2 Cut out the templates then lay them on to a sheet of mounting board; trace around the edges with a pencil. Cut the number of pieces indicated on each template: when assembled they will form a casket and lid.

Forming the casket

1 Take the front section and one side of the casket and fix together with small strips of masking tape. Add the other side and back in the same way. Once you have assembled the rectangular box reinforce the corners with lengths of masking tape.

2 Measure 1.2cm (¹⁄₂in) in from the edges of the base and draw a rectangle in pencil: this is a guide for fixing the casket sides.

3 Apply PVA glue along the bottom edge of the rectangular box and place it centrally on to the base: use your pencil line to make sure the box is in position. Hold the two sections firmly together, then leave to dry for an hour.

4 Glue the two long insert strips along the inside of the front and back edges of the

casket, with 1.2cm (¹⁄₂in) protruding above the top of the sides: this will give a ledge for the lid to sit over. Repeat for the two shorter sides.

Making the lid

1 Using the templates on pages 33 and 34, cut the lid and two lid ends from mounting board. Score the lid in the places marked by the dotted lines on the trace using a blunt knife; fold on the scored lines.

2 Apply a layer of PVA glue along the top edge of one lid end piece. Place the scored and folded lid over the lid end, holding it in place with strips of masking tape. Repeat for the other side, then check that the lid fits before leaving it to dry.

Applying the papier mâché

1 Tear strips of newspaper into 4x2cm (1¹⁄₂x³⁄₄in) pieces. Mix equal quantities of PVA glue and water in a container.

2 Brush the PVA glue mix on to a small area on the outside of the casket. Place a piece of newspaper over the glued area then brush over with more glue, removing any bubbles or creases that appear. Add more newspaper pieces,

overlapping the edges until the outside of the
casket base is covered. Press the paper well
around the rim of the casket, so that the lid
will fit; leave to dry overnight. Repeat for
the inside and outside of the lid then leave to
dry overnight.

3 Cut four 10cm (4in) squares of aluminium
foil and scrunch into balls. Turn the casket
upside down and apply circles of PVA glue
2.5cm (1in) from each corner on the base. Press
a foil ball on to each glue circle to make feet.

4 Apply a second layer of papier mâché strips
over the casket, the foil feet and the lid.

5 When dry, paint the inside and outside of
the casket and lid with white emulsion,
then leave to dry.

Applying the tissue paper

1 Cut the tissue giftwrap into diamond shapes
using the template on page 33.

2 Mix equal quantities of PVA glue and water
in a container, then brush a thin coat on to
one side of the casket; apply a tissue
diamond over the glue. Brush on more PVA
and position another diamond partly covering
the first; as you work use the brush to smooth
out any air bubbles that may have appeared

under the tissue. Be careful as the wet tissue paper can stick to your fingers and pull off the casket. If necessary work on very small sections, leaving the tissue to dry for an hour before adding more diamonds. Keep adding tissue until the surface of the lid and casket are covered: the tissue paper should go inside the casket but no lower than the rim inserts. Leave to dry overnight.

3 If any of the diamond edges have become unstuck refix with a tiny amount of PVA glue. Allow to dry, then apply three coats of matt acrylic varnish for protection.

4 Using the templates for the decorative panels on page 35, cut two small and three large panels from gold tissue paper. Secure a small panel on to each side of the casket, and a large panel on to the front, back and lid using PVA glue.

5 With an almost dry brush highlight the edges of the casket with gold acrylic paint.

6 Using PVA glue fix a length of gold braid around the bottom edge of the lid. Thread a needle with fine gold thread and attach beads and charms to the braid at the corners and the midway points.

7 Glue a painted heart in the centre of each gold tissue panel.

Making the card and gift tag

1 Cut a circle of gold card larger than your papier mâché rose. Glue the gold circle to the front of the greetings card, then edge the circle with gold braid. Stick the painted rose on to the centre of the circle using PVA glue.

2 To make the gift tag: glue a painted rose on to a parcel label, then thread with gold ribbon.

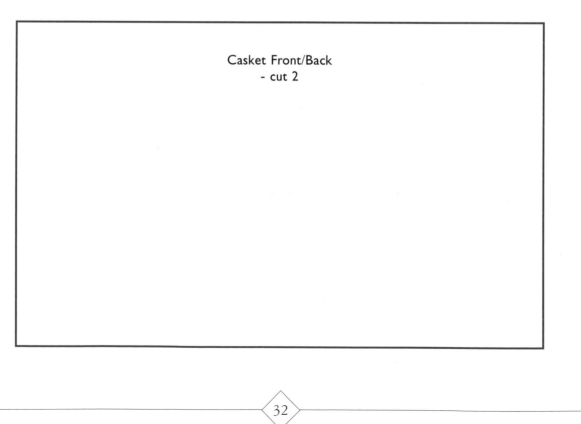

Casket Front/Back
- cut 2

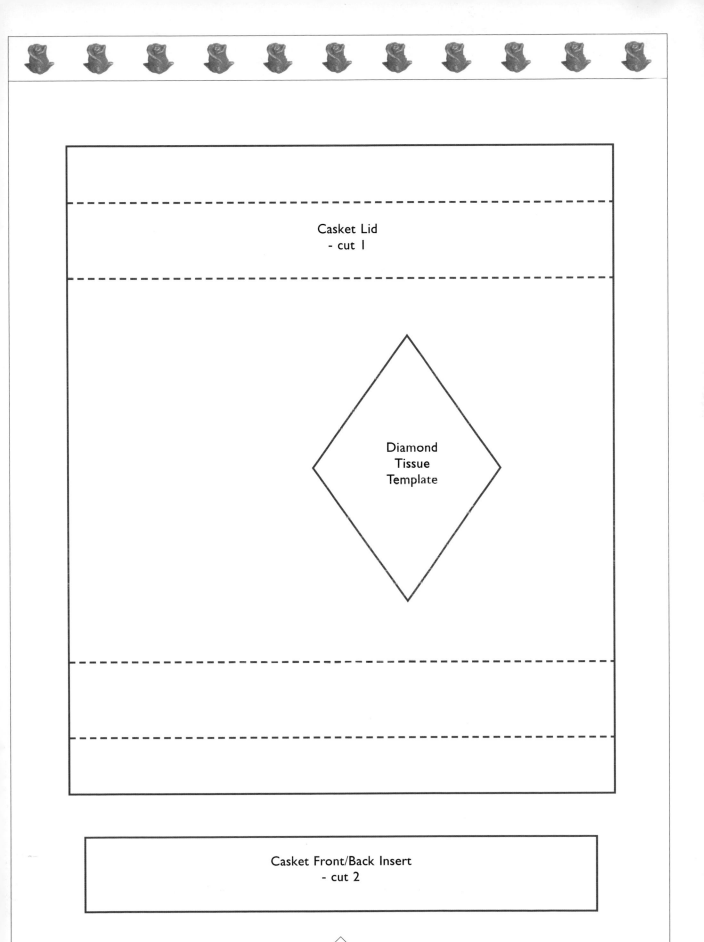

Casket Lid
- cut 1

Diamond
Tissue
Template

Casket Front/Back Insert
- cut 2

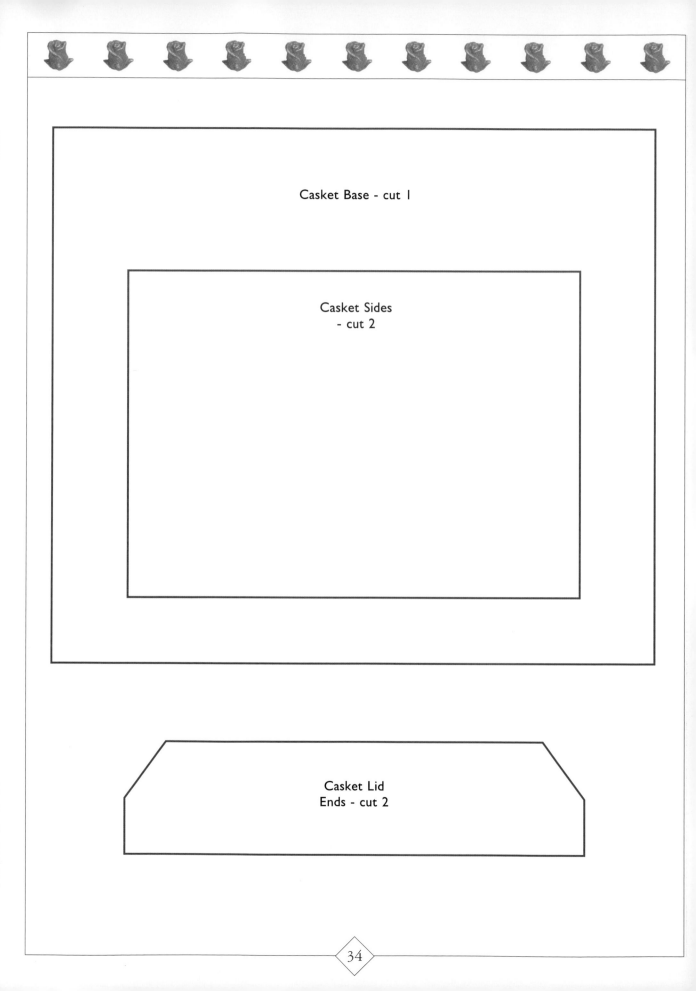

Casket Base - cut 1

Casket Sides
- cut 2

Casket Lid
Ends - cut 2

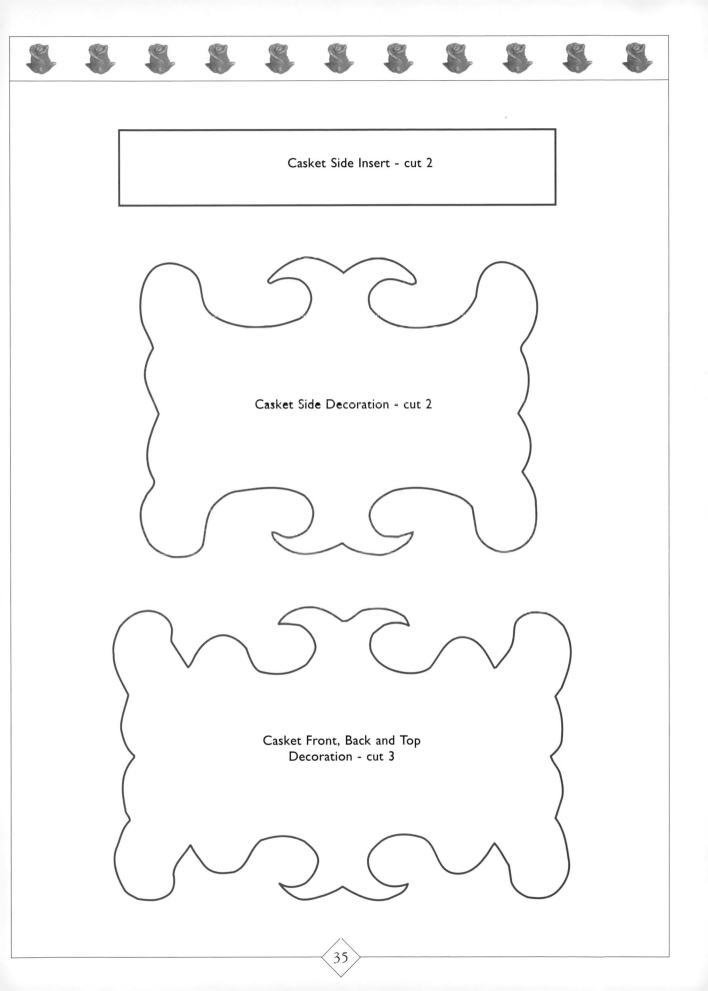

Casket Side Insert - cut 2

Casket Side Decoration - cut 2

Casket Front, Back and Top
Decoration - cut 3

Novelty Jewellery

This novelty jewellery made from paper and card is sure to get you noticed when worn on a plain black sweater or dress. The jewellery is easy to make and will cost you next to nothing as the layers are torn from old newspaper then covered with scraps of giftwrap

You will need

- Corrugated card
- Giftwrap
- Newspaper
- PVA glue, water, container for mixing glue
- Flat-backed glass jewellery stones – round and heart shaped
- Outliner paste – gold, dark pink, pink, green, pale green
- Small pair of pliers, scissors
- Two 8mm ($5/16$in) diameter beads
- Two headpins – jewellery findings
- Two earring wires – jewellery findings
- Pencil, white paper
- Brooch pin, stick pin
- Craft knife, paintbrush
- Superglue, thick needle

Tracing the design

1 Make a tracing of the templates on page 39 on to white paper. Using scissors carefully cut around the outlines.

2 Lay the tracings on to corrugated card and draw around the outside with a pencil. Cut out the corrugated card shapes using scissors: one hand, one stick pin and two earring shapes. The cardboard shapes are used as a base for building up the papier mâché layers.

Covering with papier mâché

1 Tear newspaper into strips of between 6mm ($1/4$in) and 1.2cm ($1/2$in) wide.

2 Mix PVA glue with a little water until it is the consistency of single cream.

3 Brush the PVA solution on to the newspaper strips and smooth them over the corrugated cardboard shapes. Apply three layers of paper, laying each in a different direction, overlapping the edges of the pieces, and folding the newspaper over the cardboard edges for a neat finish. Place the jewellery on a cake rack and leave to dry overnight.

4 When dry, cover the newspaper with a final layer of papier mâché using strips of giftwrap paper. Cover both sides of the jewellery, finishing with a 6mm ($1/4$in) wide

strip of giftwrap paper around the edges to neaten them. Smooth out any air bubbles, taking care that the pattern does not come off.

5 Paint a coat of the PVA solution over both sides of each piece of jewellery to seal it; leave to dry.

Finishing the earrings

1 Using PVA glue fix a red jewel in the bottom centre of each earring.

2 Apply a line around the jewel using gold outliner paste. Squeeze the tube of outliner paste gently, keeping your hand steady, as if using an icing tube. Add dots and wavy lines in dark pink, pink, green and gold outliner paste, following the photograph for position; leave to dry overnight.

3 Use a thick needle to make a hole through the earrings, entering and emerging on the side of the earrings at the points shown on the trace on the opposite page.

4 Insert a headpin upwards through the hole in each earring then thread on a bead,

leaving the rounded pin head on the lower edge. Cut the headpin 8mm (⁵/₁₆in) above the bead and bend it round into a loop using a pair of pliers.

5 Fix an earring wire on to the top of the loop; repeat for the other earring.

Finishing the brooch

1 Glue a large pink jewel on to the centre bottom of the hand shape; and a heart shaped jewel on to one of the fingers.

2 Using gold outliner paste draw around the jewels. Use pink to draw swirls on each finger, and gold, pink and green to draw wavy lines and dots.

3 Use superglue to stick a brooch pin on to the centre back of the brooch.

Finishing the stick pin

1 Using PVA, attach a large jewel to the centre of the stick pin.

2 Using the gold outliner paste outline the jewel then add a swirly line to its face; leave to dry. Use pale green and pink to add dots and lines to the stick pin using the photograph for position; leave to dry.

3 Make a hole with a thick needle at the bottom end of the stick pin. Dab superglue on the point of the metal pin and push it into the hole in the stick pin; leave to dry. Push the cap over the sharp end of the pin.

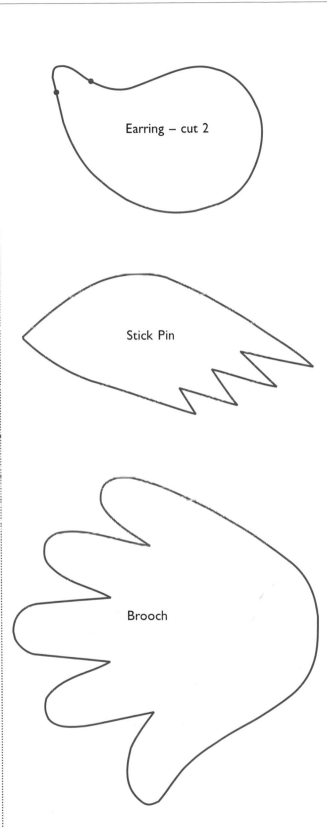

Earring – cut 2

Stick Pin

Brooch

Use these tracings to make your own jewellery shapes.

Classical Urn and Vase

To give this urn and vase strength, a conical-shaped lampshade has been used as a base for the project. Almost any size and shape of lampshade can be used, as long as the metal framework can be removed from the covering. Newspaper strips are then pasted over the shade and the surface painted and decorated with stars

If your finished urn or vase is top heavy, put small pebbles in the bottom before filling it.

You will need
- Conical-shaped paper lampshade
- Newspaper
- Thin card
- Corrugated card
- PVA glue
- Textured handmade paper
- Acrylic paint – blue
- Craft paint – silver, gold
- Acrylic varnish – matt
- Stiff cardboard, stencil brush
- Container for mixing glue
- Glue brush

Preparing the lampshade

1 Remove the metal frame from inside the lampshade: this is usually glued in place and can be eased away from the shade using a blunt knife or screwdriver. If the shade gets damaged it can be repaired when the papier mâché is applied.

2 Place the smaller end of the shade on to thin card and draw around with a pencil, then cut out the card circle. Place the card circle over the smaller end of the shade. Use PVA glue and short strips of paper to attach it to the shade. Stick the paper smoothly over the join between the base and the shade. Leave to dry.

Making the urn

1 Tear the newspaper into strips 2.5cm (1in) wide. Mix the PVA glue with a little water until it is the consistency of single cream.

2 Brush the PVA solution on to a newspaper strip and smooth it on the prepared lampshade. Continue applying strips inside and outside, overlapping the edges of the paper. Apply two layers of paper strips which should be laid in a different direction. Leave to dry, which may take several days.

3 Cut four handles from corrugated card using the template on page 17. Using the PVA solution, glue the handles in pairs, squeezing the edges of the card together. Apply one layer of papier mâché strips to the handles.

4 Attach the handles to each side of the urn using short strips of paper, in the same way as for the base. Apply another seven layers of papier mâché to the outside of the urn, including the handles.

5 For the final layer glue strips of textured handmade paper inside and outside of the urn. Cut the lower edge of the textured paper level with the base. Leave to dry.

6 Paint the outside surface of the urn blue, leave to dry. Paint the handles and inside the urn gold, taking care where the blue and gold meet.

7 Make a small star-shaped stencil from stiff cardboard using the template opposite as a guide. Load a stencil brush with silver paint then dab it on to paper to remove most of the paint. Holding the stencil firmly on to the front of the urn, lightly dab the silver paint in the cut-out area of the stencil. Remove the stencil

and reposition on the pot. Stencil several more stars either side of the first, then dab silver and gold paint lightly around the stars with the stencil brush. When the paint is dry, seal the urn inside and out with a coat of matt acrylic varnish.

Making the vase

1 Prepare the vase in the same way as the urn, removing the frame and adding a base.

2 Cover the vase, inside and outside with two layers of pasted newspaper strips in the same way as for the urn, and leave to dry.

3 Apply seven more layers of papier mâché on to the outside of the pot. Allow to dry then cover the inside and outside of the vase with textured paper in the same way as the urn.

4 Paint the outside of the vase using gold paint and the inside silver. Cut a star from corrugated card using the template on this page, then paint the front and cut edges using silver, leave to dry. Glue the star to the centre front of the vase; seal with matt acrylic varnish.

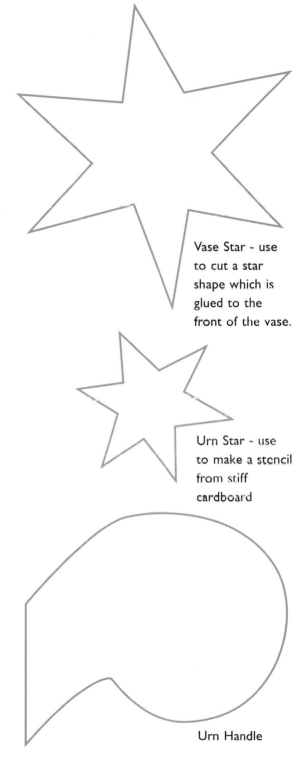

Vase Star - use to cut a star shape which is glued to the front of the vase.

Urn Star - use to make a stencil from stiff cardboard

Urn Handle

Use these outlines to make handles for the urn and to decorate the urn and vase with stars.

St Basil's Desk Tidy

Echoing the stunning and distinctive rooftops of Moscow, this novel tidy
will bring the classic shapes of St Basil's cathedral to your desk top. Beneath
the shapely towers are cardboard tubes, providing ideal storage for pens,
pencils and paper clips

You will need a selection of cardboard tubes in
various widths and lengths for this project:
packing tubes, the inside of paper rolls, toilet
tissue, clingfilm or aluminium foil.

You will need

- Ready-mixed papier mâché pulp or white
  cartridge paper and PVA glue
- 2mm mounting board
- Cardboard tubes
- Thin cardboard
- Gloss acrylic paint – brick red, blue, red, green,
  yellow, white
- Primer – white undercoat
- Metallic paint – gold
- Aluminium baking foil
- Heavy-duty craft knife, cutting mat
- Bradawl, pencil
- PVA glue
- Fine sandpaper
- Wood screws

Cutting the tubes

1 Following the plan on page 49, cut five
buildings from cardboard tubes, and five
circular lid sections. You can use a ruler and
pencil to mark the cutting line around each
tube, or attach a pencil horizontally to the top

of a box or other similar object of the right
height, and turn the tube whilst holding it
against the pencil: this will give a level line
around the tube. Sand the cut edges until each
section will stand flat on the table.

Assembling the lids

1 Lay the five lid sections on to 2mm
mounting board and draw around each. The
diameter of the tubes can be different, as long
as you remember that all the pieces for each
building and lid must be the same. Cut out the

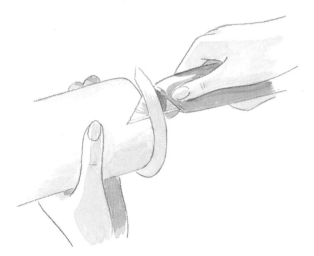

five discs, slightly larger than the pencil lines, then glue them to the ends of the lid sections.

2 After the glue has dried, carefully trim off the excess card using a sharp knife. Use a bradawl to make a hole in the centre of each disc.

Making the conical tower

1 Cut a pencil to a length of 10cm (4in). Sharpen both ends then glue one end into the hole in the top of a lid section. Leave the glue to dry (see diagram below).

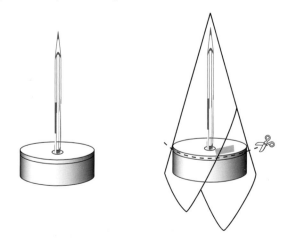

2 Bend a sheet of A4 card into a conical 'megaphone' shape to fit over the pencil; tape it together. Draw a line on the inside of the cone where the edges of the cardboard overlap. Remove the tape, then draw another line 6mm (¼in) away from the first. Cut along the second line: this will be the overlap when gluing the cone together. Roll the card into a cone and glue together on the overlap.

3 The base of the cone will still be shaped like the sheet of cardboard that you started with. To cut it level, position the cone over the lid and cut off most of the excess card, leaving a slight overlap. Apply glue around the top edge of the lid, and to the top of the pencil. Place the cone in position and leave to dry. Carefully trim off any excess card around the base with a craft knife (see diagram). To hide the join line in the cardboard, glue a further two layers of thin card over it, cutting the card so that the edges butt up to one another rather than overlapping.

Making the dome lids

1 Scrunch up aluminium foil in to a ball, then flatten one side. Position the foil ball on to a lid section: the ball should not overlap the edges as when covered in papier mâché it will form the core section of the domed lid.

2 Make up a batch of papier mâché pulp (see Making Paper Pulp, page 8). To do this, tear up white cartridge paper into strips and then soak overnight in a bowl of water. Add more water to the mix and then use a blender or liquidizer to break down the paper into a pulp. Strain the pulp over a bowl to remove the excess water: the pulp should be damp but stiff enough to be moulded over the foil. Add PVA glue to the sieved pulp using your hands, in the proportions of approximately 15g (½oz) glue to 250g (½lb) pulp.

3 Paint the foil with a coat of neat PVA glue. Before the glue has dried, apply the first

layer of papier mâché over the entire surface of the foil; check at regular intervals to make sure the covered foil dome is not getting too large to fit the lid section. Surface smoothness is not a priority at this stage - the idea is just to get the shape of each onion dome as well as you can. Make a tiny dome (without a foil centre) to fit on the top of the conical tower. Leave to dry in a warm place.

4 Sand the surface of each dome and then apply a second coat of papier mâché, this time aiming for a smooth even finish.

5 Position each dome on to its corresponding lid section, fixing it in place with PVA and a woodscrew positioned through the hole in the centre of each disc. Glue the tiny dome on to the top of the conical tower.

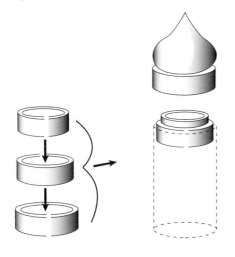

6 As they are, the lids can easily be knocked off the buildings: to keep them in place make a lip that each lid will locate on to. To do this, cut three thin strips of cardboard that fit inside the rim of each building tube. The first strip is glued level with the rim; the second and third are fixed in position with 6mm (1/4in) protruding above the rim (see diagram).

Forming the base

1 Cut a piece of 2mm cardboard approximately 20x14cm (8x5 1/2in). Position the building tubes on to the card, leaving a gap at the front between the tubes for a note pad. Mark around each tube with a pencil, then cut the board, slightly larger than the area covered by the tubes. Cut another piece of cardboard the same size and glue the two pieces together.

2 Apply two coats of white undercoat to the base, the buildings and the lids taking care to apply it thinly over the rims and the inside edge of each lid. When the undercoat is dry, paint the base and the outside of each building tube with brick red acrylic.

Painting the domes

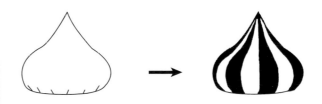

1 To paint the blue and white dome: mark a dot with a pencil at a point near the base of the dome, then mark a corresponding point on the opposite side of the dome. Keep dividing the sections in half until the dome is divided into 16 equal parts. Draw a line from each of these points to the tip of the dome. Paint the stripes with blue and white acrylic.

started. Paint in the stripes with green and yellow acrylic.

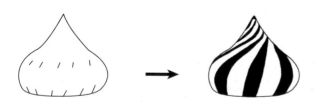

2 To paint the green and yellow dome: mark points around the base as before, but this time mark 16 points around the middle of the dome as well. Join each dot at the base to a dot four points further around on the middle row, then continue the line until it joins the top of the dome on the opposite side to where it

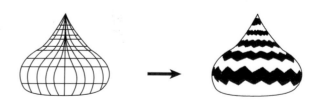

3 To paint the red and white dome: mark equally spaced dots around the dome and then draw lines from the base up to the top of the dome. Draw lines around the dome every 6mm (¼in) working up from the base to the

top. Using the grid as a guide, mark in the zigzag lines which go laterally around the dome, using a pencil. Paint using red and white gloss acrylics.

Applying the gold decoration

1 Paint the tiny dome, the tip of each painted dome and the edges of the rims and building tubes with three coats of gold metallic paint.

2 The decorative detail lines are all applied in stages: firstly the tube rims and the horizontal lines are painted gold and white – these can be painted by resting the brush horizontally on a box and turning the tube while keeping it in contact with the brush.

When the paint is dry, add the vertical lines and the arches in gold and white. Finally using the photograph opposite for position, fill in the detail to the buildings and lids using white, red, blue and yellow.

Assembling the structure

1 Glue each tube in position on to the baseboard using PVA: hold the tubes in position until the glue is dry and wipe away any glue that squeezes out around the edge with a damp cloth.

2 For extra protection, paint the structure inside and out with a coat of gloss varnish. When dry add a notepad to the base, and fill with pens and pencils.

Use this plan as a guide for cutting and positioning the building tubes and rooftops. You can vary the height and size of the tubes depending on what you will be storing in them.

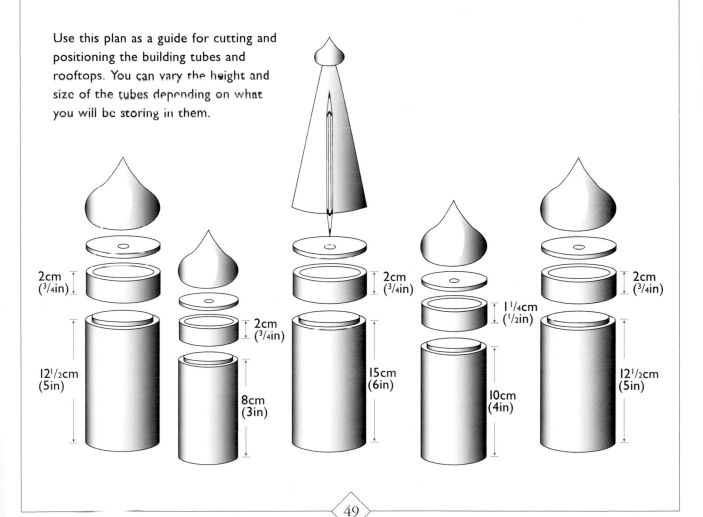

2cm (³/₄in)

12½cm (5in)

2cm (³/₄in)

8cm (3in)

2cm (³/₄in)

15cm (6in)

1¼cm (½in)

10cm (4in)

2cm (³/₄in)

12½cm (5in)

Gift Bowls

These fun gift bowls are simple to make from either white or coloured papier mâché, which can be dyed or painted. Use ready-mixed pulp for speed, or make your own from cartridge paper and PVA glue. Once dry the bowls can be filled with goodies, wrapped in cellophane, then decorated with ribbon

You will need

- Ready-mixed papier mâché pulp or white cartridge paper and PVA glue
- Cartridge paper – blue, yellow
- Cold water fabric dye – green, pink, light blue
- Acrylic paint – pink, yellow
- Paintbrush
- Hot water
- Bowl for moulding – china or plastic
- Bowl for mixing pulp
- Petroleum jelly, tablespoon, double-sided tape
- Cloth, clingfilm, rubber gloves
- Small container for mixing dye
- Acrylic varnish – matt

Preparing the moulds

1 Apply a thin coating of petroleum jelly over the surface of a china or plastic bowl, then wrap the bowl in clingfilm: the jelly will hold the clingfilm in place while you are applying the papier mâché.

Making papier mâché

1 To make the bowls you can use ready-mixed paper pulp which you can colour with dye; you can make your own pulp from white paper, which can then be dyed; or you can make the pulp from coloured paper (see Making Paper Pulp, page 8).

2 To make your own pulp, tear up strips of white, yellow or blue cartridge paper and soak overnight in a bowl of water. Add plenty of water to the mix then use a blender or liquidizer to break it down into pulp (see Making Paper Pulp, page 8).

3 Strain the pulp to remove the excess water, then mix with a small quantity of PVA glue.

Making dyed paper pulp

1 Make up a batch of white paper pulp following the instructions for making paper pulp above. Wearing rubber gloves, sprinkle an amount of cold water fabric dye into a container, add a teaspoon of hot water and mix with a spoon.

bowl. Do not apply the pulp too thickly, or the finished bowl will be heavy and chunky.

2 Pour a small amount of the dye on to the papier mâché pulp and mix thoroughly. Do not add too much liquid to the pulp or it will become sticky and unworkable. It is better to dilute the powdered dye in a little water, as when dry the pulp will be a much lighter shade. Wrap the coloured pulps individually in cling film: the pulp will keep for several days if stored in the refrigerator.

Making the tulip bowl

1 Make a quantity of papier mâché pulp in light blue, pink and green, using dye or coloured paper.

2 Using the template opposite, cut enough tulip shapes from white paper to fit around the bowl you will be using as a mould. Secure the tulips evenly around the outside of the bowl using double-sided tape. Lightly coat the outer surface of the bowl with petroleum jelly, the wrap in cling film. Place the prepared bowl upside down on a larger upturned dish.

3 Make the tulip stems with green pulp and the tulip heads with pink. To apply the pulp to the bowl: pick up a small amount in your hand and squeeze out the excess water, then press the pulp firmly on to the side of the

Fill in the background in light blue: cover the base first, then work up the sides smoothing the colours together where they meet. Continue adding blue pulp until the sides of the bowl are covered. Allow to dry for three days then carefully remove the mould and peel away the clingfilm. It will be several more days until the bowl is completely dry.

Making the blue star bowl

1 Make a quantity of papier mâché pulp in yellow and blue, using dye or coloured paper (see Making Paper Pulp, page 8).

2 Trace over the star shape opposite on to white paper and cut out the template. For this project the bowl is built inside another bowl, so you will need a clear bowl. Using double-sided tape, fix the template to the bottom of the bowl, with the star points coming up the sides.

3 Lightly coat the inside of the bowl with petroleum jelly, then line with cling film.

4 Apply pieces of yellow pulp over the star template in the bottom of the bowl. Work up the points until the star shape is covered.

5 Fill the background of the bowl with blue papier mâché, blending it where the blue and yellow meet. When the pulp is two thirds of the way up the sides of the bowl add yellow spots, made from 1.2cm (½in) balls of pulp. Press each ball on to the side of the bowl and then flatten. Add blue pulp around the yellow spots, blending the edges together with your finger as you work. Complete the bowl, then allow to dry for three days. Carefully remove from the mould then peel away the clingfilm. Leave until completely dry.

Making the pink star bowl

1 Line the inside of your mould with clingfilm as for the blue star bowl.

2 Make a quantity of white paper pulp, then press the pulp thinly over the inside surface of the mould.

3 Leave to dry for several days then remove from the mould. Remove the clingfilm and leave until completely dry.

4 Place the star template on the bottom of the bowl and lightly draw around it with a pencil. Paint the star with yellow, and the bowl with pink acrylic paint.

Sealing the bowls

1 When the papier mâché bowls are dry, seal the surface with matt acrylic varnish.

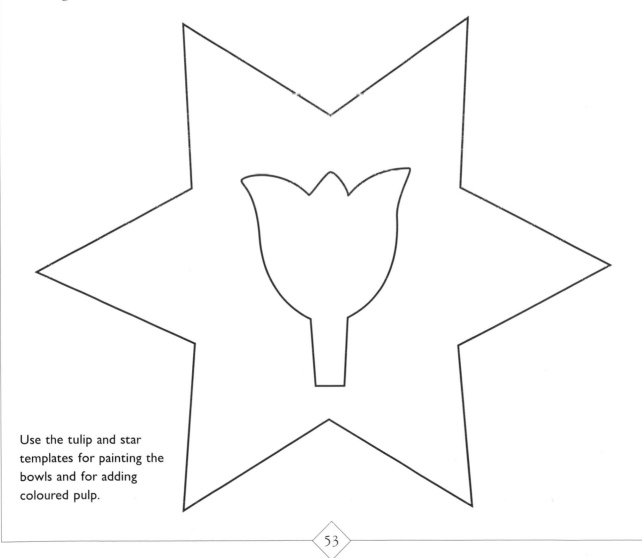

Use the tulip and star templates for painting the bowls and for adding coloured pulp.

Vegetable Caskets

Choose a firm, under-ripe pepper or aubergine as a mould for this project. The paper layers are built over the vegetable, then when dry the paper vegetable is cut in half and the real vegetable removed. A brass hinge is then added making a useful gift box for sweets or chocolates

You will need

- Aubergine or pepper
- White emulsion or acrylic gesso
- Acrylic paint – purple, red, green, gold
- Newspaper
- Petroleum jelly
- PVA glue
- Interior wood filler
- Fine sandpaper
- Craft knife
- Water-based gloss varnish
- 2cm (³⁄₄in) brass hinge
- Thick needle
- Fine brass wire
- Two brass paper fasteners
- Hook fastening

Choosing your vegetable

1 As you will be using a vegetable as a mould for the papier mâché layers, choose one that is a good solid shape, firm and not over-ripe. Almost any fruit or vegetable can be used, but remember when choosing, the more interesting the shape of the vegetable the better the shape of the finished casket will be.

2 Smear your pepper or aubergine liberally with petroleum jelly: this will act as a releasing agent when you remove the vegetable from the mould.

Applying the papier mâché

1 Tear newspaper into strips 6mm (¹⁄₄in) to 1.5cm (⁵⁄₈in) wide, and 5cm (2in) long. Mix 3 parts PVA glue to 1 part water until it is the consistency of single cream.

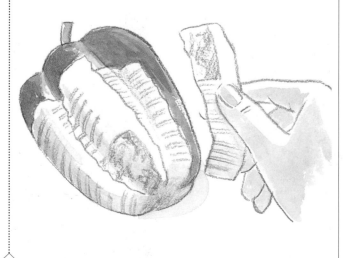

3 Paste the PVA solution on to a newspaper strip and then smooth it on to the vegetable mould. Continue applying strips of paper, overlapping the edges of the paper pieces as you work. Apply 10 layers in all, placing each layer in a different direction. Alternating black and white and coloured newspaper strips will enable you to see the different layers more easily. Leave the papier mâché to dry overnight.

4 To make the paper vegetable look like the real thing: use wood filler to fill in any irregularities, then when dry, lightly sand the surface to get a smooth even finish. Place the paper vegetable on to the table and check that it will stand in the correct position: add more filler and sand until you are happy that the casket is level.

Removing the vegetable

1 Draw a pencil line around the widest part of the papier mâché vegetable. Using a sharp knife carefully cut through the papier mâché layer working around the drawn line: do not cut the vegetable, or the juice may leak into the papier mâché. Carefully pull the two halves of the mould apart and gently remove the vegetable (see diagram on page 56).

Painting the casket

1 Undercoat the casket inside and out with two coats of white emulsion or acrylic gesso, leaving to dry between coats.

2 Paint both halves of the casket on the inside with two coats of gold, leaving them to dry between coats.

3 Paint the outside of the vegetable casket with two coats of acrylic paint in a colour much brighter than the real vegetable: pillar box red for the pepper and mauve for the aubergine. Take care on the top edges where the colour meets the gold to get a neat line. When dry, paint the stalk area of the vegetable green. Paint the inside and outside of the casket with two coats of gloss varnish.

Assembling the casket

1 Hold the two sections of the casket together and place the hinge over the join at the back.

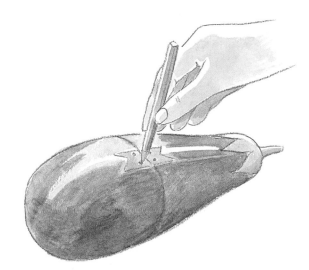

2 Mark the position of the fixing holes on both parts using a felt-tipped pen, then using a thick needle, pierce through the papier mâché layer at these points.

3 Cut two 5cm (2in) lengths of fine brass wire. Bend one in the middle and insert the ends through one half of the hinge, then through the holes on one section of the casket and twist the wire ends together inside the casket. Attach the hinge to the other end of the casket in the same way.

4 At the front of the casket, make a hole 6mm (¼in) above the join on the top half. Slip the pronged end of a brass paper fastener through the hole in the hook fastening. Insert the prongs through the hole and splay them open on the inside: although the hook is held firmly, it should have enough slack to turn and engage with the fastener at the bottom.

5 Make a hole at the front of the casket on the lower section and attach a brass paper fastener in the same way as before.

6 Fill the casket with tissue paper and a selection of brightly wrapped chocolates.

Medieval Bowl and Card

A pear-shaped balloon has been used as a mould to construct this traditional shaped bowl: layers of newspaper are glued on to the balloon, which is then popped. To give the bowl a rough medieval look, papier mâché pulp is smeared on to the outside, before adding decoration using paint and cord

You will need

- Newspaper
- Papier mâché pulp
- Fine handmade paper – red
- Pear-shaped balloon
- Thin card, mounting board
- PVA glue, masking tape
- Thick card 12.5x25cm (5x10in), or a greetings card blank to fit the design – violet
- Cord – gold, violet
- Craft paint – silver, gold
- Acrylic paint – red, orange, apricot
- Acrylic gesso or white emulsion paint
- Craft wax – gold
- Container for mixing glue, skewer
- Glue brush, paintbrush

Making the bowl base

1 To make the base cut a strip of thin card 32x3cm (12³⁄₄ x 1¹⁄₄in). Bend into a ring overlapping the ends then tape together with masking tape. Draw around the ring on to thin card and cut out the circle. Attach the circle to the bottom of the ring with masking tape.

Applying the papier mâché

1 Tear newspaper into strips about 1.5cm (⁵⁄₈in) wide. Tear these strips into 5cm (2in) lengths. Mix PVA glue in a container with a little water. Paste strips of paper to overlap the join between the ring and the base circle, using PVA solution; leave to dry.

2 Blow up the balloon and sit it wide end down into the ring. Apply five layers of

pasted newspaper strips to the base and lower third of the balloon. Leave to dry.

3 Pop the balloon and remove it from the bowl, then using sharp scissors cut the upper edge of the bowl level. Cut seven 3cm (1¼in) lengths of gold cord. Apply a dab of PVA glue on each end of the cord to prevent it from fraying. Divide the distance around the base into seven, then glue the cord pieces vertically around the base using PVA glue.

4 Make a quantity of papier mâché using ready-mixed paper pulp or make your own paper pulp (see Making Paper Pulp, page 8). Brush the thinned PVA solution on to the outside of the bowl and press a 6mm (¼in) thick layer of papier mâché pulp on top. Add a thicker band of pulp around the rim. Using a skewer make twelve holes evenly around the bowl, just under the rim: the holes must be large enough to take the coloured cord. Leave the bowl to dry for at least 24 hours.

Painting the bowl

1 Paint the bowl with an undercoat of white emulsion paint or acrylic gesso, taking care not to paint the gold cord on the base. When dry, paint the base, rim and 2cm (¾in) inside the bowl red; inside of the bowl gold, and a blend of orange and apricot over the outer surface.

2 Draw four arches evenly on the outside of the bowl, using the template on page 61 as a guide. Tear fine handmade red paper into

strips and apply to the inside of the arches using the thinned PVA solution. When the paint is dry, rub the bowl all over with gold wax.

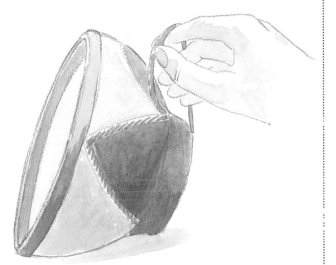

Adding the cord

1 Glue violet cord along the edges of the arches using PVA glue. If you do not have violet cord, paint white or cream cord with violet acrylic paint thinned with a little water.

2 Using the template on the right as a guide, paint a row of fleur-de-lys shapes freehand in gold, around the inside of the bowl.

3 Paint the mounting board gold. When dry, use the template on the right to cut twelve diamonds from the card; paint the cut edges with gold. Glue three diamonds to each arched section of the bowl, following the photograph.

4 Thread violet cord through the holes in the side of the bowl, then tie the ends together in a knot.

Making the card

1 Press papier mâché pulp into a 10cm (4in) square, making it 8mm (⁵⁄₁₆in) thick and

the surface reasonably flat; leave to dry. Using the template below, cut an arch shape from white paper. Lay this on to the dry pulp and cut out the shape using a sharp knife. Paint the arch red then rub with gold wax.

2 Score a rectangle of card across the centre then fold in half widthways to make a card large enough to take the arch. Glue the painted arch to the card front. Starting at the top, glue gold cord around the arch shape; cut the cord ends at an angle so that they fit together at the top.

3 From the gold mounting board cut three more diamond shapes; glue them to the papier mâché arch. Paint a row of freehand fleur-de-lys shapes along the base of the card, below the arch, using gold paint.

Fleur-de-lys Template

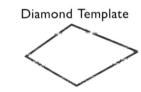

Diamond Template

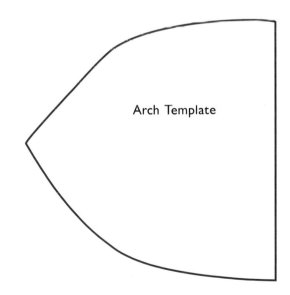

Arch Template

Use the arch, diamond and fleur-de-lys templates to decorate the bowl and card.

Acknowledgements

Thanks to the designers for contributing such wonderful projects:
Sunflowers and Vase (page 14), Lynn Strange and Susan Penny
Caribbean Platter and Bowl (page 20), Amanda Joseph
Native American Trays (page 24), Cheryl Owen
Rose Casket and Card (page 28), Lynn Strange and Susan Penny
Novelty Jewellery (page 36), Cheryl Owen
Classical Urn and Vase (page 40), Cheryl Owen
St Basil's Desk Tidy (page 44), Michael Ball
Gift Bowls (page 50), Lynn Strange
Vegetable Caskets (page 54), Cheryl Owen
Medieval Bowl and Cards (page 58), Cheryl Owen

Many thanks to Jon Stone for his inspirational photography.

Other books in the Made Easy series

3-D Découpage (David & Charles, 1999)

Mosaics (David & Charles, 1999)

Ceramic Painting (David & Charles, 1999)

Stamping (David & Charles, 1998)

Stencilling (David & Charles, 1998)

Glass Painting (David & Charles, 1998)

Silk Painting (David & Charles, 1998)

Suppliers

Craft World (Head office only)
No 8 North Street
Guildford
Surrey GU1 4AF
Tel: 07000 757070
Retail shops nationwide, telephone for local
store
(Craft warehouse)

Dylon International Ltd
Consumer Advise Bureau
Worsley Bridge Road
Lower Sydenham
London SE26 5HD
Tel: 0181 663 4296
Telephone for your local retail stockist or send
SAE for free consumer advice on dyeing
(Cold water fabric dye)

Hobby Crafts (Head office only)
River Court, Southern Sector
Bournemouth International Airport
Christchurch
Dorset BH23 6SE
Tel: 0800 272387 freephone
Retail shops nationwide, telephone for local
store
(Craft warehouse)

Homecrafts Direct
PO Box 38
Leicester LE1 9BU
Tel: 0116 251 3139
Mail order service
(Craft supplies)

Index

Page numbers in *italics* refer to main photograph

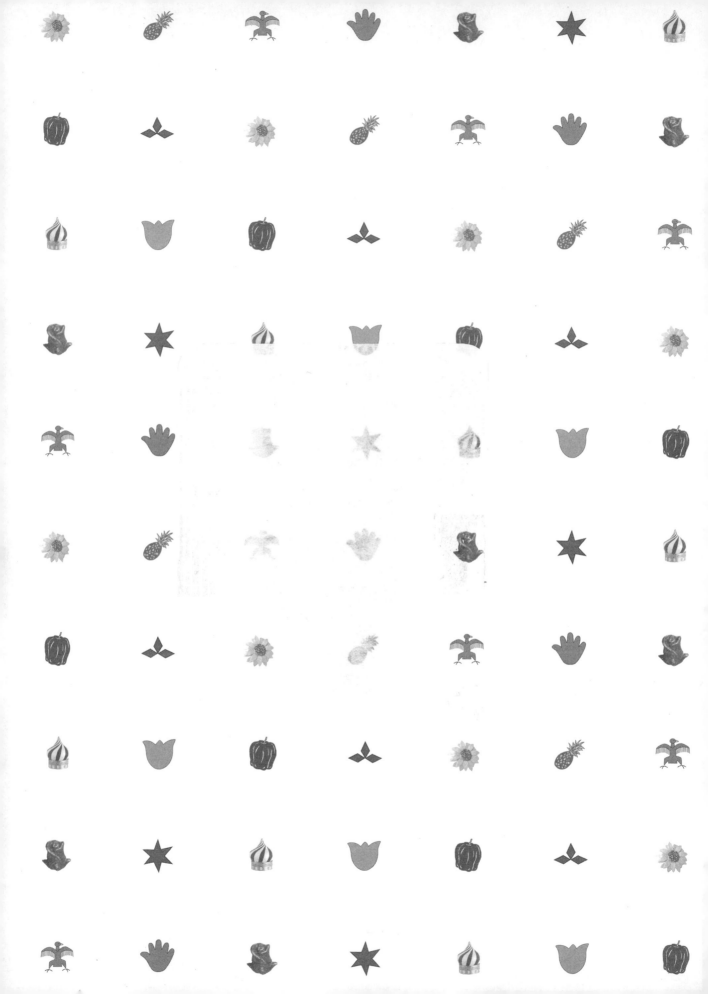